Dear Parent:
Your child's love _____ here!

Every child learns to read in a different way and at his or her own

_____ ls and read
_____ each level in
_____ become more
_____ d abilities. From
_____ e or she reads
_____ reading:

_____ al illustrations,

_____ oncepts

_____ age play

_____ gh-interest topics

_____ nes

_____ e joy of reading
_____ trators and a
_____ s set the

A lifetime of discovery begins with the magical words "I Can Read!"

Visit www.icanread.com for information
on enriching your child's reading experience.

A Good King is Hard to Find

First published in Great Britain in 2007 by HarperCollins Children's Books.
HarperCollins Children's Books is a division of HarperCollins Publishers Ltd.

1 3 5 7 9 10 8 6 4 2

ISBN-13: 978-0-00-724827-8
ISBN-10: 0-00-724827-X

Shrek the Third: A Good King is Hard to Find.

Printed and bound in Belgium

I Can Read!

READING 2 WITH HELP

DREAMWORKS
SHREK THE THIRD

A Good King is Hard to Find

Adapted by Catherine Hapka
Illustrations by Steven E. Gordon

HarperCollins *Children's Books*

The kingdom of Far Far Away
needs a new king.
Shrek and Fiona are next in line
for the throne.

But Shrek does not want the job.
"There must be somebody else,"
he says.
"Anybody?"

There's only one way out.

Shrek must find Fiona's cousin,

a kid named Arthur Pendragon.

Artie can be king instead.

Shrek says good-bye to Fiona
and sets off on another adventure
with his best friends,
Donkey and Puss In Boots.

Soon they find Artie.

He doesn't look much like a king,

but Shrek doesn't care.

"Come on, Your Majesty," says Shrek.

"Let's get you fitted for your crown."

His classmates laugh.

"King?" they say.

"More like the Mayor of Loserville!"

Artie turns toward the crowd.

"So long, guys," he says.

"Have fun in class while I run a kingdom."

Artie follows Shrek onto the ship.

They set sail for Far Far Away.

"You'll love being king,"
Shrek tells Artie.
"You'll have chefs making you fancy food,"
says Donkey.

"And you'll have royal tasters
so you won't get poisoned," Puss adds.
"Your royal bodyguards will keep you safe,"
says Donkey.
"Poison? Bodyguards? Stop the boat!"
yells Artie.

Artie grabs the wheel

to turn the ship around.

"I'm going back!" he cries.

"Back to being a loser?" Shrek asks.

Then he feels terrible.

Shrek and Artie fight to control the ship. They end up crashing it instead.

When they get to shore,
the group finds an old wizard
named Merlin.
He used to be Artie's teacher.

Merlin performs a magic spell.
It sends Artie and the others
straight back to Far Far Away.

Shrek thinks his problems are over.

Then he gets a look at Far Far Away.

The evil Prince Charming

has almost taken over the kingdom.

Artie thinks the city looks terrible.
"It wasn't like this when we left,"
Shrek tells him.

They find Shrek's friend, Pinocchio.

"The villains have taken over!" he says.

Pinocchio points to a poster for a play.

The poster shows Charming defeating Shrek.

Shrek and his friends

talk their way into the castle.

They have to stop Charming!

Shrek and Artie find Prince Charming.

Charming laughs at Artie.

Artie turns to Shrek.

"Go away, kid.

There's nothing you can do," says Shrek.

After Artie leaves the room,

Charming captures Shrek.

It's almost time for the play to start!

"Ladies and gentlemen,"
Charming says to the crowd.
"Welcome to my happily-ever-after."
He points his sword at Shrek.

A bright light hits the stage.

"Hold it!" yells Artie from above.

He grabs a rope and swings to the floor.

Charming and his villains want to fight.

But Artie has a better idea.

"Do you really want to be villains
forever?" he asks the bad guys.

"Don't you ever wish
you could be something else?"

The villains like what they hear.

They turn against Charming.

Now Charming will never be king!

Artie used to feel like a loser.

But now he feels smart and strong.

Maybe he is fit to be king, after all.

Shrek holds out the crown.

"It's yours if you want it,"

he tells Artie.

"But this time, it's your choice."

Artie smiles and puts on the crown.

His new subjects cheer and shout.

"Artie! Artie! Artie!"

yells the crowd.